FEMALE HEROES OF GREEK MYTHOLOGY

FEMALE HEROES OF GREEK MYTHOLOGY

Goddesses, mortals, muses, and more!

MEGAN DUVARNEY FORBES

ILLUSTRATIONS BY MEEL TAMPHANON

Illustrations by Meel Tamphanon
Author photo courtesy of Jillian Rae
Series Designer: Brian Lewis
Art Director: Angela Navarra
Art Producer: Stacey Stambaugh
Editor: Kristen Depken
Production Editor: Rachel Taenzler
Production Designer: Martin Worthington

Published by Callisto Publishing LLC C/O Sourcebooks LLC
P.O. Box 4410, Naperville, Illinois 60567-4410
(630) 961-3900
callistopublishing.com

Library of Congress Cataloging-in-Publication Data is on file with the publisher.

This product conforms to all applicable CPSC and CPSIA standards.

Source of Production: 1010 Printing Asia Limited, Kwun Tong, Hong Kong, China
Date of Production: July 2025
Run Number: 5044654

Printed and bound in China.
OGP 10 9 8 7 6 5 4 3 2 1

To my favorite little goddesses,
Moriah and Audrey

CONTENTS

INTRODUCTION

Greek myths have been passed down from generation to generation for thousands of years. In the past, they helped the ancient Greeks understand and organize the world around them. Today, they teach us about what life was like in the ancient world and about the power of storytelling. Many of the most popular stories of ancient Greece are about men like Heracles, Perseus, and Zeus. But this book is about the female heroes whose stories are just as important. If we want to understand life in the ancient world, we can't silence half of the characters. These stories of the female heroes teach us about the strength, bravery, mistakes, and fears of the women in Greek mythology.

You'll learn about Rhea, who saved her children with a magic potion, and Leto, who turned evil men into frogs. Women like Atalanta and the Amazons were fierce warriors. Queen Penelope of Ithaca and Queen Helen of Sparta played major roles in one of the most famous wars in history, the Trojan War. For you readers who are already fans of Greek mythology, pay attention to how familiar myths sometimes take on a different meaning from a female perspective. How do the themes change when we hear from the voices that are often silenced? Now, sit back and enjoy the stories of these 51 fabulous women and goddesses!

GAIA

The Earth

Gaia is the goddess of the earth and the mother of all life. She was one of the very first **deities** in Greek mythology.

According to Greek tradition, the beginning of time was marked by chaos and darkness. Within this darkness, everything that exists now existed, but it was a mass of confusion.

Gaia was the earth, and Ouranos was the sky. They married and created a separation between the heavens and the earth, which organized the universe. Gaia and Ouranos had eighteen children. Twelve of them were beautiful, and they became the gods and goddesses called the **Titans**. The other six children were monsters who had either one eye or one hundred arms.

Ouranos hated his six monster children and banished them into a dark pit below the earth called Tartarus. Gaia loved all her children, and she was furious at Ouranos for what he did. She conspired with her youngest Titan son, Cronos, to get revenge on Ouranos and free her other children from Tartarus.

Cronos slashed his father with a knife, overthrew him, and became king of the gods.

Gaia continued to protect the children of cruel fathers. She had a **prophecy** that, because Cronos had overthrown his father, one of his children would also overthrow him. Cronos was terrified that Gaia's prophecy would come true. His wife, the goddess Rhea, gave birth to many children. Cronos ate them as soon as they were born.

But when his son Zeus was born, Gaia helped Rhea trick Cronos into eating a rock wrapped in a blanket instead. Gaia secretly raised Zeus to protect him.

The ancient Greeks worshipped Gaia as the goddess of the earth and the mother of all living things. She is the first goddess, and she bestowed powers to the goddesses who came after her. Stories of goddesses similar to Gaia have been found in other areas, such as Turkey and India.

DID YOU KNOW?

A space telescope launched in 2013 was named Gaia, after the Greek goddess. Its mission is to create the most accurate 3-D model of space, with nearly a billion stars, planets, and asteroids.

SYMBOLS

Gaia is clothed in mountains and ocean.

RHEA

Mother Goddess

Rhea is one of the first mothers in Greek mythology. She went to great lengths to rescue her children from their father, Cronos.

Rhea was the daughter of Gaia and Ouranos, who represented earth and heaven. Rhea was a Titan goddess of comfort and ease. But her life was not always comfortable or easy.

Gaia had prophesied that one of Cronos's children would overthrow him, so every time Rhea had a child, Cronos ate the baby. When Rhea became pregnant for the sixth time, she and Gaia worked together to save the baby from Cronos.

Rhea traveled to the island of Crete and set up a nursery for herself and her baby in a cozy cave. She gave birth to a son named Zeus, and Cronos immediately came to the cave to see his son. When Cronos arrived, Rhea greeted him with her new baby, wrapped snugly in a soft blanket. Cronos snatched the baby from her and popped it in his mouth!

But Rhea had played a trick on Cronos. Instead of the baby, she had actually wrapped a rock in the blanket. The real baby Zeus was safe and sound inside the cave. **Nymphs** were babysitting him and feeding him with goat milk, keeping him quiet so that Cronos wouldn't hear him cry.

While Rhea was happy to have saved Zeus, she also had a plan to rescue her other five children. Years later, when Zeus was grown up, Rhea brought Cronos a sweet drink for dessert. Gaia had given her a potion to mix in it to make him throw up. Cronos got so sick that he threw up the first five children that he had eaten: Hestia, Demeter, Hera, Hades, and Poseidon.

These young gods teamed up with Gaia's monster children who had been banished to Tartarus. Together, they overthrew Cronos, and Zeus became king of the gods.

DID YOU KNOW?

The island of Crete, where Rhea escaped to give birth to Zeus, is the largest island in Greece and has the largest population.

SYMBOLS

Rhea is usually carrying a swaddled baby.

APHRODITE

Goddess of Love

Aphrodite was the most beautiful of the goddesses. As the goddess of love, she played matchmaker for many humans and fell in love with several gods.

Back when Cronos slashed his father Ouranos, some of Ouranos's blood splashed into the sea. The blood mixed with sea-foam, and out of the foam, Aphrodite was born. She emerged from the ocean in a giant seashell. She then joined the Olympian gods as the goddess of love and romance.

Aphrodite was married to Hephaestus, the god of fire and blacksmiths, but Aphrodite couldn't help but get caught up in other romances wherever she went. Her true love was Ares, the god of war. They had a son together named Eros, who became the god of love.

Because Aphrodite loved romance and parties, she attended the wedding of a sea nymph named Thetis and a **mortal** king named Peleus. Aphrodite held a goblet of ambrosia, the gods' favorite drink. She mingled with the other lovely goddesses, Hera and Athena.

The goddess of chaos, Eris, had not been invited to the wedding. Suddenly, she appeared and rolled a golden apple toward Aphrodite, Hera, and Athena. The words "For the fairest" were etched into the apple. Whoever was the most beautiful should have the golden apple, and all three of the goddesses wanted it.

Zeus did not want to anger any of the goddesses by choosing a winner in this competition, so he selected a Trojan prince named Paris to name the most beautiful goddess. Hera, the queen of the gods, surrounded by peacocks, promised Paris wealth and power if he chose her. Athena, the goddess of warfare, promised him glory on the battlefield. Aphrodite, always thinking of love, promised him the most beautiful mortal woman on earth as his wife.

Aphrodite's offer was the most tempting to Paris. He gave her the golden apple, officially designating her the most beautiful goddess of them all. She accepted the title and flaunted her beauty everywhere she went.

DID YOU KNOW?

In the middle of summer, ancient Greeks held a festival of love honoring Aphrodite, similar to a Valentine's Day party today. The celebration was all about love!

SYMBOLS

Aphrodite is associated with seashells, red roses, doves, and golden apples.

HESTIA

Goddess of the Hearth

Hestia stayed out of most of the drama and conflict that Greek gods are known for. However, she was the goddess the ancient Greeks greeted every morning when they woke up and started a fire to make their breakfast.

Hestia was the goddess of the **hearth**, or the fireplace in ancient homes. Every time someone used their hearth to heat their home, cook their food, or forge a tool, they thanked the goddess Hestia.

Hestia was the oldest child of Cronos and Rhea. Poseidon and Apollo, the gods of the sea and the sun, both wanted to marry her, but she refused them both and chose to live the single life. She didn't have children and liked to stay home instead of interacting with the other gods.

Still, she was the most highly honored goddess on Mount Olympus. She received more **sacrifices** than the rest of the gods put together! This is because ancient Greeks offered sacrifices by burning meat or grain for the god they wanted to honor. To start the fire, they had to pray to Hestia. So every time any god received a sacrifice, Hestia got one first.

Hestia is associated with the cozy rituals of homelife. As ancient Greeks baked bread and heated water for their meals together, they gave thanks to Hestia. Bread and kettles were often used as symbols for her.

Unlike the rest of her fellow Olympian gods, Hestia did not have conflicts with other gods or with humans. There are no stories about her getting revenge on a mortal out of jealousy, or turning humans into animals—this is very rare for a god!

She was roommates with the messenger god Hermes, who was often traveling to deliver messages for other gods. Hestia maintained the home and the hearth fire while he was away. We can picture her sitting by the fireplace, reading a book, drinking her tea, enjoying her alone time.

The next time you cozy up next to a warm fireplace, think of the kind goddess Hestia.

DID YOU KNOW?

Ancient Greeks had a saying: "To start with Hestia," which meant "to start from the beginning." This is probably because ancient Greeks honored Hestia at the beginning of every sacrifice.

SYMBOLS

Hestia is associated with fire, bread, and kettles.

METIS

Goddess of Wisdom and Advice

Metis was a goddess known for her good advice. She was the daughter of Oceanus and Tethys, Titan descendants of Gaia and Ouranos. Other gods often came to Metis when they had problems.

When Zeus and Rhea were trying to find a way to rescue Zeus's siblings from Cronos's stomach, they knew they should ask Metis. She came up with the plan to give Cronos a potion that would make him throw up the other children he had swallowed. She gave the potion to Gaia, and then Gaia gave it to Cronos.

Metis caught Zeus's eye after this, and he wanted to marry her. At first Metis had no interest in Zeus and she tried to escape from his advances. She turned into a bird so that she could fly away from him, and then into a lion to try to fight him off. She also turned herself into a deer so that she could sprint away and hide in the forest. Later on, though, she married Zeus and became pregnant.

Gaia warned Zeus that, just like his father, he would have a child more powerful than he was. He decided not to take any chances, so he went one step further than his father Cronos did. Instead of waiting until Metis had her baby, he simply swallowed Metis whole!

Metis gave birth while she was still inside Zeus, and Zeus developed a terrible headache. He held on to his head and groaned in pain. It felt like something was kicking the inside of his skull.

Zeus asked Hephaestus, the god of blacksmithing, to help him. This probably wasn't the best god to go to for medical advice. Hephaestus was holding an axe he had just made, so he hit Zeus in the head with it.

Zeus's head cracked open, and out came the goddess Athena, fully grown and wearing body armor.

Metis faded from Greek mythology stories after this, but her daughter Athena went on to be a very influential and powerful goddess.

DID YOU KNOW?

Although Hera is famously the wife of Zeus, Metis was known as his first wife. Metis and Hera were also both raised by Oceanus and Tethys.

SYMBOLS

Metis is associated with owls and olive trees.

DEMETER

Goddess of the Harvest

Demeter was the goddess of grain, the most important resource in the human world. But what was most important to Demeter was her daughter, Persephone.

Demeter was another daughter of Rhea and Cronos, and she had her daughter, Persephone, with Zeus. Humans were dependent on her for a good harvest of grain and other crops. They offered sacrifices to her as gifts, hoping for success with their fields.

One day, Persephone went to play in a meadow with her friends. She noticed a beautiful flower and leaned toward it to smell it. Suddenly, the earth opened beneath her, and she vanished.

Demeter searched everywhere for her daughter, but no one knew where she was. Demeter refused to eat or drink or bathe. Ten days later, the goddess Hecate told Demeter that she had found Persephone. Hades, the god of the **underworld**, had kidnapped her. Hades was too powerful to defeat, so there was nothing they could do. Demeter was overcome with grief.

Demeter abandoned Mount Olympus and disguised herself as an old woman on earth. She took a job as a nanny for a baby boy because the boy's mother, Iambe, told funny jokes and made Demeter laugh. Being around the baby and his loving family made Demeter feel a little bit better.

Absorbed in her new job, Demeter let the crops and other plants on earth die. Zeus was not happy about this. He told Demeter he would help her bring Persephone back to earth if she would restore the crops.

A servant named Ascalaphus pointed out that it was against the rules for Persephone to go back to earth because Hades had secretly fed Persephone a pomegranate seed. Demeter angrily dropped a large rock on Ascalaphus and killed him. Zeus winced and then compromised. He said that Persephone could live with Demeter on earth for nine months of the year, and she would have to spend the other three months in the underworld. Demeter agreed to this deal and restored the crops and flowers to the earth again.

DID YOU KNOW?

Near the city of Naxos in Greece, there is a marble **temple** that was dedicated to Demeter. It is still in very good condition, even though it is about 1,500 years old!

SYMBOLS

Demeter is associated with cornucopias, torches, and wheat.

HERA

Queen of the Gods

Hera was the most powerful of the goddesses and a fierce protector of the people she loved. If you got on her bad side, watch out!

Hera was another child of Cronos and Rhea, but she was raised by foster parents named Oceanus and Tethys. Hera especially loved her foster mother, Tethys, and would go back to visit her often.

Hera married Zeus, the king of the gods. She was the goddess of marriage and protector of brides. But it was difficult to be married to Zeus for all eternity. He was not faithful to Hera, and even though he was **immortal**, he never got any better at being a good husband.

Sometimes Hera tried to punish Zeus by turning his girlfriends into animals. She turned mortal women into cranes, cows, cats, and bears. She could also turn herself into different animals to trick Zeus or anyone else who wronged her. Most often, she turned herself into a peacock, a lion, or a cow.

Hera's most famous enemy was a baby. Zeus had a son with a mortal woman named Alcmene. Alcmene named the baby Heracles, meaning "glory of Hera" to try to get Hera to like him. This did not work. Hera continued to try to punish Heracles (also known as Hercules) as he grew up. Because of Hera's tricks, Heracles had to perform twelve labors, or challenges, and he became famous throughout Greece.

Zeus and Hera also had sons and daughters of their own. Two important descendants were Ares and Enyo, the god and goddess of war. Hera always involved herself in wars and did everything she could to help Greek heroes.

Hera also had a daughter named Eileithyia, the goddess of childbirth. For ancient Greek women, marriage and childbirth would have been two of the most important aspects of their lives. They would have called on Hera and Eileithyia to help them through some of their happiest and most difficult days.

Hera was the most important goddess to the ancient Greeks, and they dedicated many beautiful temples to her.

DID YOU KNOW?

The torch for the Olympic Games is still lit in the ruins of Hera's temple in Olympia to this day.

SYMBOLS

Hera is associated with crowns, lotus flowers, and peacocks.

✳ THE FATES ✳

Goddesses of Destiny

The Fates were three sisters who determined how long each human was going to live. They were the daughters of Zeus and Themis, the goddess of divine order.

Clotho was the Spinner. When a woman was pregnant, Clotho would begin weaving a thread that represented the baby's life.

Lachesis determined how long the thread would be. If a person lived a long life, they had a long thread. She also chose how much struggle they would experience in their lifetime. This was shown in the texture of the thread.

Finally, Atropos was in charge of cutting the thread at the end of a person's life. Her name meant "stubborn" or "unshakable," because no one could talk her out of cutting someone's thread when the time came. She also chose how a person would die. Some people were meant to die as a hero in battle, while others died of disease or old age.

Sometimes the Fates were shown as old women with hunched backs and stern faces. At other times, they were shown as young goddesses. They were always women, however, because women were in charge of bringing life into the world. Women were also in charge of weaving. In ancient Greece, women, weaving, and birth were all interconnected.

The Fates also attended the births of gods and gave them prophecies about what their powers would be. For example, the Fates were there when Athena was born from Zeus's head, and they told her that she would not marry or have children. Instead, they told her she would have power in war and wisdom.

The Fates had their own power that was unique from both humans and other gods. Humans had their own free will, and gods had their powers, but neither of them could change what the Fates determined.

While the ancient Greeks offered sacrifices and dedicated temples to many of the gods, they knew that the will of the Fates could not be changed. The Fates determined a person's destiny, and the ancient Greeks accepted whatever they decided.

DID YOU KNOW?

The ancient Greeks believed that the Fates put a certain amount of good and evil in each person. For centuries, humans have tried to understand why people do good or bad things, and this was one explanation.

SYMBOLS

The Fates are associated with thread, measuring rods, and scissors.

PANDORA

The First Woman

The first human woman brought hope into the world. Her name was Pandora.

On Mount Olympus, Zeus instructed Hephaestus, the god of blacksmithing, to take a lump of clay and shape it into the first woman. Hephaestus made a beautiful statue. Aphrodite gave the figure deep emotion, and Hermes gave her a voice. Athena gave her the talent to weave, while Zeus gave her curiosity. They named her Pandora, which means "the all-gifted one."

Zeus had one more gift for her. He handed her a jar and told her that it contained many precious things. Pandora thanked him and immediately began to imagine all the wondrous things that could be inside. Athena, the goddess of wisdom, pulled her aside.

"Never, ever open this jar, Pandora," Athena warned her. "Do not look at what is inside." Pandora nodded and followed Hermes to her new home on earth.

There she met two brothers named Prometheus, who was very cautious, and Epimetheus, who often acted without thinking.

Epimetheus fell in love with Pandora at first sight and wanted to marry her. Prometheus, on the other hand, was suspicious of a gift from Zeus, even if it was a beautiful woman.

Pandora loved her new life on earth with her husband Epimetheus, but she kept wondering what was inside her jar. After all, Zeus had given her the gift of curiosity. One day, she couldn't take it any longer. She cautiously opened the lid.

Out flew ten thousand horrible creatures that carried plague, famine, disasters, and evil.

"No!" Pandora cried. She shoved the lid back into place, sobbing with the knowledge of what she had done. Prometheus had been right to be suspicious; Zeus's plan all along was to bring pain into the world through Pandora.

But Pandora's quick actions stopped the worst of the creatures from escaping. Despair was still trapped in the jar. She released a warm beam of light and gave her own gift to the world: hope in the face of sadness.

DID YOU KNOW?

Several ancient cultures have stories about the first woman being tricked into bringing evil into the world. Can you think of any others?

SYMBOLS

Pandora is associated with a magic jar or box from Zeus.

STYX

Goddess of the Underworld and Oaths

Styx was one of the Titan goddesses, born into a family with a lot of drama. She had to choose sides in a family fight, and was rewarded for her choice.

Styx was the daughter of Tethys and Oceanus, the beautiful children of Gaia and Ouranos. Styx's uncle Cronos had been at war with his son Zeus for control of Mount Olympus.

In this War of the Titans, Styx's generation of gods was fighting against the younger generation, the Olympians. Zeus led the Olympians, and Cronos led the Titans. Zeus's siblings, like Hades, Hera, and Poseidon, joined him. Most of the Titans fought alongside Cronos.

The Olympians won the war, and the first thing Zeus did was punish the Titans who had fought against him. Most of them were imprisoned in Tartarus, located so far beneath the earth that it was beneath the underworld. Poseidon built bronze gates to trap them inside. One Titan named Atlas was punished by being forced to hold up the sky for eternity. Ancient people often depicted him as a man on one knee, struggling to hold up a giant globe.

Styx, however, had been the first Titan to switch sides and pledge her allegiance to Zeus. Because of her oath, Zeus commanded that all promises in the future would be made in her name. If any gods broke a promise, she would punish them.

Styx lived at the entrance of the underworld and took the form of a river. She contained one-tenth as much water as her father, Oceanus, who wrapped around the entire earth. If a god wanted to make an oath, the goddess Iris would go to Styx, scoop up a goblet of water, and bring it back to the god to swear upon.

The goddess Styx had four children named Zelus, Nike, Kratos, and Bia. While people in modern times often associate her with death, her most important role in Greek mythology was to uphold promises.

EXPLORE MORE!

The Ancient Greeks believed that the River Styx trickled into earth in an area called Arcadia. The stream was thought to be poisonous.

SYMBOLS

Styx is associated with rivers and oaths.

* THE FURIES *

Goddesses of Justice

The Furies were fierce protectors of families. Anyone who hurt one of their own family members lived in fear of their punishment, but everyone else was safe from the wrath of the Furies.

Like Aphrodite, the Furies were born from Ouranos's spilled blood. While Aphrodite came from the mix of his blood and the sea, the Furies came from the mix of his blood and the earth. The three sisters always traveled together. Their names were Alecto, Megaera, and Tisiphone.

The Furies had snakes wrapped around their hair and arms, and they sometimes had blood dripping from their eyes. They wore black dresses and had belts around their waists and sandals on their feet. However, most people could not see them. They would only appear to the people they were going to punish.

The Furies came from the underworld, and they decided who was guilty of crimes. Mortals and other gods could not stop them, no matter how hard they tried. The Furies spoke as a group, all three sisters declaring that someone was guilty in unison. They would kill the guilty person who had harmed their family.

Although the Furies were terrifying to anyone who had committed a crime against a family member, there were others who had the chance to see them in a different light. A man named Orpheus descended into the underworld to search for his wife. He sang a song so beautiful that the Furies burst into tears and cried for his lost love. Even Athena once called them "the kind ones."

In ancient Greece, fear of the Furies was an important part of holding society together. Men and husbands had many more rights than women and children, but powerful men still feared the wrath of the three sisters. In a world where women and children were rarely protected, sometimes stories were the best way to ensure that people did not commit crimes against their families.

DID YOU KNOW?

If you and your friends are ever in need of a costume idea, dress as Furies! Wear black dresses, add a belt and some sandals, and wrap toy snakes around your wrists like bracelets.

SYMBOLS

The Furies are associated with snakes.

LETO

Goddess of Motherhood

Leto gave up everything to bring her twins into the world. The ancient Greeks worshipped her as the goddess of motherhood.

Leto lived among the other gods, goddesses, and Titans on Mount Olympus. She was known as a very modest goddess. She did not like to draw attention to herself, and in images of Leto, she is often lowering a veil over her face.

Zeus decided that he liked Leto, and she became pregnant by him. Zeus's wife Hera was furious. She banished Leto to the earth and told the humans that if anyone helped her, they would be cursed as well.

Leto wandered the earth, pregnant and alone. She was exhausted and thirsty when she came upon a stream. She rushed to it with cupped hands.

Some local men saw her and recognized her as the pregnant woman Hera had told them about. They refused to let her drink. She tried to push past them, but they jumped in the stream and kicked up the mud so that the water was undrinkable.

Remembering that she was still a goddess, Leto stood up straight and pointed directly at the men. Their skin turned green and bumpy, they grew webs between their fingers, and they shrunk down to the mud. She had turned them into frogs! The only word they could say from now on was "Ribbit!"

Leto still needed to find a place to give birth. Zeus, feeling guilty about getting her banished, sent a dolphin to carry her to a floating island called Delos. There, she lay under a palm tree and gave birth to twins: the goddess Artemis and the god Apollo.

Leto was a goddess, but now she knew what it was like to give birth on earth. She had both a daughter and a son. Ancient Greek women honored her as the goddess of motherhood because they felt a connection to her story and believed they could trust her to help them through the journey of motherhood.

DID YOU KNOW?

If you want to see how the ancient Greeks pictured Leto, you can look at an ancient Greek vase with Leto, Artemis, and Apollo painted on it. It is currently in the British Museum, and you can see it on their website.

SYMBOLS

Leto is associated with veils, palm trees, and wolves.

ATHENA

Goddess of War and Wisdom

Athena emerged fully grown—and fully dressed in battle armor—from Zeus's head. She loved to help Greeks in war.

Zeus was thrilled when Athena was born. Because she was a girl, she could not overthrow him. He tried to get her to marry Hephaestus, whose axe had set her free from Zeus's head. But Athena did not want to marry anyone. She was Zeus's favorite child, so he agreed that she could stay single, giving her more time to help Greek heroes in battle. She was the goddess of war.

One of Athena's favorite Greek heroes was Odysseus. She helped Odysseus and his fellow Greeks during the Trojan War, and she continued to help him after.

Odysseus was participating in an athletic tournament, and his next event was a footrace. He offered up a prayer to Athena on the starting line, so she rushed to his aid and made his feet light and quick. But another runner named Ajax was gaining on him as they approached the finish line, so Athena stuck out her foot and tripped Ajax. He fell face-first into a pile of cow poop!

Though Athena could be ruthless, she was also very wise. She and the god of the sea, Poseidon, once had a contest to see who could create the object that was most useful to humans. Poseidon created a horse. It was beautiful, fast, and helpful to humans in many tasks.

Athena created an olive tree. Not only did it provide olives for food and oil, but its wood, twigs, and leaves were also useful. The olive tree became a symbol of peace and prosperity.

Athena won the contest, and as a reward, she named the capital city after herself. Today, Athens is still the capital of Greece, in honor of the goddess Athena.

DID YOU KNOW?

The Parthenon is an enormous temple in Greece dedicated to Athena. It used to hold a statue of her that stood over 30 feet tall, decorated with ivory and gold.

SYMBOLS

Athena is associated with owls, olive trees, spears, and helmets.

NIKE

Goddess of Victory

Nike was the personification of victory. As a goddess, she accompanied Athena, the goddess of war, into battles to ensure that they would defeat their enemies.

Nike was the daughter of the goddess Styx and the Titan god Pallas. Pallas was a god of warcraft, so his children were also associated with war. His son Zelus represented glory, Kratos represented strength, Bia represented force, and Nike represented victory.

When Nike's mother Styx pledged her allegiance to Zeus in the War of the Titans, she also brought her children along. In a battle against the monster Typhoeus, everyone else fled except for Zeus and Nike. They charged into battle. Nike shielded Zeus as he threw his thunderbolts across the sky. Together they defeated Typhoeus.

Because Nike fought alongside Zeus, she was one of his favorite goddesses. Even though she was one of the lesser gods, he arranged for her to accompany his favorite daughter, Athena.

From then on, Nike was always associated with Athena, goddess of war.

The ancient Greeks loved to decorate vases and pots with images of Nike. She had large wings and carried a palm branch. She made people feel brave. She was like a good luck charm that Greeks loved to have in their homes.

In Athens, the ancient Greeks built a beautiful temple on a hill overlooking the city. They named it the Temple of Athena Nike. There was a beautiful sculpture of Nike in the temple, reaching down to take off her sandal. Taking off sandals showed respect when entering a temple. The ancient Greeks came to the temple to worship Nike when they were hoping for victory against their enemies in war.

DID YOU KNOW?

You've probably heard of the popular shoe company called Nike. One of the founders, Jeff Johnson, said he had a dream about the goddess Nike and decided to name the company after her.

SYMBOLS

Nike is associated with palm branches (symbols of victory).

PYRRHA

Daughter of Pandora

Although Pandora was the first human woman, it was her daughter Pyrrha who made sure that humans continued to survive on earth. Pyrrha also gave birth to a son who would become the first king of the Greek people.

Pyrrha was the daughter of Pandora and her husband, Epimetheus. Pyrrha married Deucalion, the son of Prometheus (Epimetheus's brother).

Zeus had never been a big fan of humans. He had tried to trick Pandora into ruining the earth with the contents of a mysterious jar. By the time Pyrrha was an adult, Zeus was fed up with humans and decided to destroy them with a flood.

He caused a huge rainstorm to cover the earth and demolish the humans. After nine days of flooding, Zeus was sure that he had gotten rid of humans once and for all. Then, out of the corner of his eye, he saw a man and a woman in a boat. They were praying to the gods to save them. Zeus decided that since they were praying, he would allow them to live. The two people were Pyrrha and Deucalion.

They were grateful to survive, but after the waters receded, they were not sure how they were going to repopulate the earth with humans again. Deucalion remembered that once, an **oracle**, who was like a fortune teller, had told him a riddle about throwing bones behind him.

Pyrrha solved the riddle and realized that "bones" must be a symbol for stones. She and Deucalion threw stones over their shoulders and hoped that the oracle was right. Sure enough, the rocks that Pyrrha threw turned into human women, and the rocks that Deucalion threw turned into human men, enough to fill the earth with humans again.

Pyrrha and Deucalion had six children of their own. Ancient Greeks believed that one of their sons, Hellen, was the ancestor of all Greek people. In ancient times, instead of calling themselves Greeks, they called themselves Hellenes, in honor of their first king.

DID YOU KNOW?

The oldest flood tale that we have is from *The Epic of Gilgamesh*, written in ancient Mesopotamia in about 2100 BCE. There are also flood myths from Hindu literature, the Cheyenne Native American tribe, the Hebrew Bible, and other cultures from all over the world.

SYMBOLS

Pyrrha is associated with rocks and floods.

NYX

Goddess of the Night

Nyx, the goddess of the night, was one of the oldest deities in Greek mythology. She represented darkness and had power over many of the other gods.

Nyx was one of the original goddesses, like Gaia and Ouranos. She lived in the underworld with Hades during the daytime. She created her own children, including the gods of sleep, death, strife, and pain. She also created the three Fates, who were responsible for the events of every human's life and death.

Nyx flew through the black sky in a **chariot** and wore swirling dark clothes. She carried a black whip with her for protection, and to latch on to things that she wanted to take. As she flew through the night, she could also control people's dreams.

Nyx was very mysterious, and even though most gods didn't encounter her often, they knew that she was very powerful. Even Zeus, the king of the gods, feared her.

Hypnos was the god of sleep and one of Nyx's sons. One day, Hera was angry at Zeus, and she convinced Hypnos to put Zeus into a deep sleep for her. Hypnos used all his power and Zeus began to doze off, but eventually, Zeus awakened and broke Hypnos's spell over him.

Hypnos fled, but Zeus was furious and punished the gods on Mount Olympus for letting Hypnos get so close to him. Zeus searched far and wide for Hypnos, ready to give him the worst punishment.

Zeus found Hypnos in the sky and charged angrily toward him. Then Nyx came into view. She was shielding Hypnos. Zeus scurried back to Mount Olympus, not willing to anger or fight Nyx. She was too powerful and terrifying for him to face.

Nyx remained one of the most mysterious and terrifying goddesses of ancient Greece, even among the most powerful gods.

DID YOU KNOW?

Many cultures have night goddesses with interesting stories. Check out night deities from Egyptian, Aztec, Norse, Hindu, and Slavic traditions!

SYMBOLS

Nyx is associated with darkness, night, and chariots.

ARTEMIS

Goddess of Hunting

Artemis was a typical oldest daughter, taking on responsibilities to help her mother, twin brother, and eventually, all the young women in ancient Greece. She was the goddess of hunting, childbirth, and wild animals.

Artemis was born to the goddess Leto and the god Zeus. She was a twin, but she was born before her brother Apollo. Apollo took so long to come out that Artemis was old enough to help her mother deliver him. Because of this, she was known as a goddess of childbirth, and expectant mothers would pray to her.

Artemis loved the outdoors. She lived in the woods instead of on Mount Olympus with her fellow gods. She had lion cubs for pets. She wore a deerskin cloak and carried a bow and arrow for hunting.

Her friends were the wood nymphs who lived with her and helped take care of her. In return, she protected them from the male hunters who often roamed the woods.

Artemis usually did not trust the men who came to the woods to hunt, but she did become friends with Orion, who hunted with his dog Sirius. According to one version of the story, Artemis's brother Apollo did not approve of her relationship with Orion, so he set out to trick her. Like the typical younger brother that he was, he bet his sister that she couldn't hit a log floating on the lake with her arrow. Artemis rolled her eyes, swept an arrow from her quiver, and pierced the log on the lake directly in the center.

Unfortunately, the log was Orion out in the lake, floating on his back. Artemis was devastated that she had killed him, so she convinced Zeus to allow him to live among the stars. This is the constellation Orion.

Artemis did not marry or have children of her own. She was known as the protector of young girls. When Greek girls reached the age when they could get married, they would leave a childhood toy at a temple for Artemis as a sign that they were growing up.

DID YOU KNOW?

Many cultures around the world have myths that involve the Orion constellation. Research different myths from places like China, India, and the Americas.

SYMBOLS

Artemis is associated with deer, dogs, bears, and bows and arrows.

SELENE

Goddess of the Moon

Selene was a Titan goddess, the daughter of Hyperion and Theia, who were siblings of Rhea and Cronos. With her shining silver chariot, she brought the light of the moon to the sky each night.

Selene saw herself as a protector of the Olympian gods, who were like her younger siblings. She lit the way for Artemis to hunt by night. She also protected Zeus from attacks in the dark.

One night when Selene was bringing the moon into the sky, she spotted Typhoeus, a monster with huge wings and snakes growing from his shoulders. He was surging toward Zeus to try to kill him and take over Mount Olympus.

Selene stood guard at the gates of Mount Olympus as Typhoeus attacked. He threw bulls at her as he advanced. But Selene blocked each attack and drove Typhoeus away, saving Zeus.

Even though she succeeded, Selene's moon was damaged. There were craters and dents in her moon where she had blocked Typhoeus's attacks. The ancient Greeks believed that this is why the moon has dark spots on its surface.

After Selene brought the moon to the sky each night, she floated down to Mount Latmus to relax. One night, she saw a handsome shepherd named Endymion sleeping on the mountain. She immediately fell in love with him.

Endymion was supposed to be watching over his sheep, but Selene thought he looked so beautiful sleeping under the moonlight that she took care of his sheep for him every night.

Selene begged Zeus to make Endymion immortal so that he would always be as handsome as he was in that moment. Zeus said that he couldn't make Endymion immortal, but he could put him in a permanent sleep so that he would never age. Selene agreed to this plan, and every night she watches over Endymion and his sheep while he sleeps forever on Mount Latmus.

DID YOU KNOW?

The ancient Greeks did not build any temples to Selene because they could see her every night in the sky. Do you know which of the eight phases of the moon you can see in the sky tonight above your house? Check MoonGiant.com!

SYMBOLS

Selene is associated with the moon and a silver chariot.

✳ EOS ✳

Goddess of the Dawn

Three siblings were in charge of bringing in each new day and night on earth. Helios was the god of the sun, Selene was the goddess of the moon, and their sister Eos truly began each new day.

Eos was the goddess of dawn, that soft, glowing moment in the early morning when the moon fades and the sun begins to rise. She wore shimmering yellow robes that reflected the early morning light.

Eos gave birth to Eosphorus, the morning star, and named him after herself. She had other star-children named Boreas and Notus. She also created the god of the wind, Zephyr.

Although Eos had a glittering family of immortals, she also loved humans. She fell in love with a prince from Troy named Tithonus. She wanted to be with him forever, but she knew that he would die one day because he was a mortal.

She begged Zeus, the king of the gods, to grant Tithonus immortality. Zeus agreed to Eos's request. But Zeus never passed up an opportunity to play a trick on someone. Eos had forgotten to ask for Tithonus to remain young, so Zeus gave Tithonus immortality without stopping him from aging. Tithonus would always get older and older but never die.

Tithonus's body shriveled more and more each day. He eventually turned into a grasshopper, and the ancient Greeks believed that he lived forever, rubbing his grasshopper wings together in a song of sadness.

Eos and Tithonus had two sons named Emathion and Memnon. Emathion became the king of Arabia, but the Greek hero Hercules killed him when Emathion tried to steal some golden apples. Hercules gave Emathion's kingdom to his brother Memnon. Memnon was later killed by the Greek hero Achilles. In her grief, Eos refused to allow the sun to rise the next day.

DID YOU KNOW?

Compare Eos's request of Zeus to her sister Selene's request. What was similar and different about the outcomes? Did either sister get what she wanted?

SYMBOLS

Eos is associated with dawn and "rosy fingers."

HARMONIA

Goddess of Harmony and Balance

Harmonia was the goddess of harmony and balance. She could help calm any situation between friends, siblings, or husbands and wives.

However, Harmonia's own family was not very harmonious. Her mother was Aphrodite, the goddess of love. Aphrodite was married to Hephaestus, the god of blacksmithing, but Harmonia's father was Ares, the god of war. Hephaestus was not happy that his wife had a child with another god.

When Harmonia grew up and was old enough to get married, Zeus, the king of the gods, looked for someone worthy to be her husband. Zeus liked Cadmus, the founder of the famous city of Thebes.

Harmonia's father Ares knew Cadmus, too. When Cadmus was younger, an oracle told him to follow a cow with a crescent moon–shaped spot on her hide and establish a city wherever the cow laid down. This became the city of Thebes.

After his journey, Cadmus tried to drink water from a spring. There was a dragon guarding the spring, so Cadmus killed it. But the dragon belonged to Ares, so he was angry with Cadmus.

Ares made Cadmus work for eight years to make up for killing his dragon. At the end of the eight years, Ares agreed with Zeus that Cadmus should marry Harmonia. They arranged a wedding for the happy couple and invited the gods to attend.

Harmonia was peaceful and serene on her wedding day. Many gods attended her wedding and gave the couple gifts and prophecies. Hephaestus gave Harmonia a beautiful necklace that he made himself.

Unfortunately, this necklace was cursed. Hephaestus was still angry at Harmonia's mother, Aphrodite, and the necklace placed a curse on Harmonia's descendants.

While Harmonia and Cadmus were happy together, their children and grandchildren were cursed to lead unhappy lives. A few of their famous descendants were Semele, Pentheus, and Oedipus. Harmonia was able to help the ancient Greeks find harmony in their lives, but the curse was too strong for her to help her descendants.

DID YOU KNOW?

Harmonia's husband Cadmus was from Phoenicia. The Phoenicians invented the alphabet that we still use today, and the ancient Greeks believed that Cadmus brought it to Greece.

SYMBOLS

Harmonia is associated with necklaces.

SEMELE

Mother of Dionysus

Semele was the princess of Thebes, the city her father, Cadmus, had founded. She was mortal, but she would soon be swept into the family tree of the gods.

Like many young Greek women, Semele worshipped Zeus. She became a **priestess** at a temple dedicated to him. This was not an easy job. The ancient Greeks offered animal sacrifices to Zeus. Semele had to cut up a bull to present to Zeus as a sacrifice.

She was very dirty after this task, so she went to the river to bathe. At the same time, Zeus had changed himself into an eagle and was out for a leisurely flight. As he was flying above the river, he caught sight of Semele and thought she was very beautiful.

He landed on the riverbank and changed into the form of a man. He told Semele that he was actually Zeus, and she was starstruck! She was so excited to meet the god that she served in the temple. They fell in love, and Semele became pregnant.

Zeus, of course, was still married to the goddess Hera. Hera hated when Zeus snuck away with his human girlfriends, so she decided to trick Semele.

Hera took the form of a nurse who was caring for Semele during her pregnancy. She listened to Semele tell her about her boyfriend, Zeus.

"How do you know he is not lying?" Hera asked. "You should ask him to show himself to you in his divine form." Semele agreed that this was wise.

Zeus agreed to appear to her on his chariot, surrounded by clouds and lightning. Humans are not supposed to see gods in their true form. Semele was so frightened that she burst into flames, just as Hera knew she would.

Zeus could not save Semele, but he saved the baby from her womb. He cut a slit into his thigh and placed the baby inside until he was ready to be born. Dionysus, the god of wine and parties, was born from Zeus's leg.

DID YOU KNOW?

Semele's hometown of Thebes, Greece, is one of the oldest cities in the world. More than 30,000 people still live there today.

SYMBOLS

Semele is associated with bulls and grapes.

* PERSEPHONE *

Queen of the Underworld and Goddess of Spring

Persephone was the daughter of Zeus, the king of the gods, and Demeter, the goddess of the harvest. She lived a carefree life with her loving mother until one day, she was kidnapped and taken to the underworld.

Demeter and Persephone lived on the island of Sicily, where Demeter ruled over the crops of the earth. Persephone mostly hung out with her friends, like the goddesses Electra and Artemis, and played in wildflower fields. They lived near the volcano Mount Etna. One afternoon, the volcano began to stir. Its rumbling caused an earthquake and a crack in the ground.

Hades, the god of the underworld, was supposed to keep the two worlds separate. He rushed to Mount Etna to fill in the crack. That's when he saw Persephone in a nearby field picking flowers. He fell in love with her immediately and decided he must have her as his wife.

He snatched her around her waist and dragged her through the crack in the earth before quickly sealing it back up. Persephone screamed for her mother, but no one could hear her.

Demeter flew into a rage and begged the gods to help her get Persephone back. Zeus claimed that he couldn't help her, but when he saw that the crops on the earth were dying because of Demeter's sadness, he made a deal with her. He would allow Persephone to live on earth with Demeter for nine months of the year, but for three months, she would live with Hades in the underworld. The ancient Greeks believed that nothing grew in the three winter months when Demeter was mourning, but when Persephone came back to earth in the spring, flowers began to bloom again.

Persephone did not love her husband Hades, but she was still a romantic at heart. When men came to the underworld, desperate to rescue their wives, Persephone often convinced Hades to let the lovers be together and return to earth. She knew how heartbreaking it was to be separated from her loved ones.

EXPLORE MORE!

In 1621, Italian artist Gian Lorenzo Bernini created a marble statue of Persephone being kidnapped by Hades. It is considered one of the most beautiful (and terrifying!) sculptures of all time. It's located at the Borghese Gallery in Rome, Italy.

SYMBOLS

Persephone is associated with pomegranate, flowers, and grain seeds.

✳ EURYDICE ✳

True Love of Orpheus

Eurydice was a beautiful wood nymph, or a **dryad**, as the ancient Greeks would say. She lived in the forest with other nymphs who took care of trees and other living things.

Eurydice fell in love with a musician. Orpheus was the son of Apollo, the god of music and poetry. Orpheus played a magical **lyre** that Apollo had given him, and he wrote endless love songs for Eurydice.

Orpheus and Eurydice had a picture-perfect wedding. The god of marriage, Hymenaios, blessed their marriage, but he also gave them a warning. He told them that their happiness wouldn't last.

While Eurydice was enjoying her wedding reception, a shepherd named Aristaeus noticed her. He thought she was so beautiful that he tried to drag her away and keep her for himself. Orpheus and Eurydice fought him off and ran deeper into the woods to escape him.

Suddenly, Eurydice felt a sharp pain in her foot. She looked down and saw that a snake had bitten her. She fell to the ground and clutched Orpheus's hand. Orpheus tried to save her, but it was too late. Eurydice died and went to the underworld.

Orpheus was devastated and wrote beautiful songs about his heartbreak. He sang all day and night. Even the gods felt sorry for him. Apollo allowed him to see Hades, the god of the underworld.

Hades was bored with Orpheus's story, but his wife Persephone burst into tears after hearing his love songs. She convinced Hades to let Orpheus and Eurydice go back to earth and live happily ever after.

"Fine," Hades said. "But on one condition: You have to walk in front of Eurydice, and you cannot look back."

Orpheus agreed. Just as he was about to break free of the underworld, he wondered if Hades was trying to trick him. He turned his head just slightly to see Eurydice following right behind him. In that moment, Eurydice vanished back into the underworld forever.

DID YOU KNOW?

Eurydice and Orpheus's love story is one of the oldest tragedies in literature. Do you know of any other stories of lost love?

SYMBOLS

Eurydice is associated with snakes.

MAIA

Mother of Hermes

Maia was a shy nymph who preferred to live alone. But she grew to learn to use her voice and stand up for her son.

Maia was the daughter of Titans Atlas and Pleione. Atlas was punished by Zeus for siding against him in the War of the Titans, and he had to hold up the skies forever. Pleione was an ocean nymph with violet hair. She was a daughter of Oceanus and a protector of sailors. Perhaps Maia did not want the responsibilities that her parents had, so she lived by herself in a cave in Arcadia.

As hard as Maia tried to stay away from everyone, Zeus still found her. He visited her cave, and soon Maia became pregnant. She gave birth to Hermes, who would become a messenger to the gods. Hermes would also be a guide who brought souls to the underworld.

The moment Hermes was born, Maia could tell that he was different from most immortal beings. He was incredibly smart, and good at stealing. While he was still just a few days old, he snuck away and stole a herd of cattle from Apollo, the sun-god.

Apollo stormed into Maia's cave and demanded to know how his cattle ended up on her mountain. He accused Hermes of stealing the cows.

But Maia held up her tiny son, who was swaddled in blankets, and said, "You think this baby stole your cattle? He's only a few days old! How could he possibly do such a thing?" Maia knew that Hermes *did* steal the cows, but she had to think quickly to get Apollo out of her cave.

Unlike Maia, Hermes liked to be the center of attention. He was a gifted musician and invented an instrument that became a part of many mythological stories, the lyre. It was like a small harp, and Hermes sang beautiful songs while he played.

Though Maia was a shy nymph, she raised a son who went on to play a major role in many ancient Greek myths.

DID YOU KNOW?

If you have ever seen an image of a Greek god with little wings on the back of his shoes, that one is Hermes! He usually carries a bag and an invisibility cloak.

SYMBOLS

Maia is associated with caves.

IRIS

Goddess of the Rainbow

In Greek, the name Iris sounds like the word for "rainbow" and the word for "messenger." The goddess Iris was associated with both rainbows and messages.

If you were a Greek citizen looking out at the coastline after it rained, you would often see a rainbow arching out from the clouds and descending into the sea. This is Iris, goddess of the rainbow, taking messages from the gods on Mount Olympus to gods on earth or in the underworld.

If any god made an oath or a promise to another god, Iris would take her golden pitcher and fly to the edge of the underworld. She would fill her pitcher from the River Styx (the goddess of oaths) and bring it back to the god for them to swear upon. This is what made the oath official to the gods.

Iris was also known as a personal messenger for Hera, the queen of the gods. Iris had golden wings on her ankles, like the other messenger god, Hermes.

Iris wore a long golden dress and always carried her pitcher in case she needed to gather water from Styx. Iris's sisters were the Harpies, who had wings and birdlike bodies. They were messengers for Hera's husband Zeus, but he usually only sent them to his enemies.

While Iris had three sisters, her mother Electra had three thousand! Electra was the child of Tethys and Oceanus, who had three thousand water nymph daughters. The whole family was associated with water, and Iris continues this tradition by revealing herself in her beautiful multicolored way after every rain.

DID YOU KNOW?

You can find very rare "lunar rainbows," or rainbows that you can see in the dark, at Victoria Falls, located on the border of Zambia and Zimbabwe.

SYMBOLS

Iris is associated with rainbows and a golden pitcher.

✳ ARACHNE ✳

The Best Weaver in Greece

Even though Arachne was not a goddess, her godlike weaving skills made her famous in her hometown of Hypaepa in Lydia, which is in modern-day Turkey.

The people of Hypaepa loved to watch Arachne weave. She used thread and a loom to create tapestries that looked like paintings. The nymphs loved to gather around and watch her create detailed scenes from simple thread.

Arachne was proud of her tapestries. Many of her pieces included threads of the deep purple shades that her father sold far and wide. Arachne and her father worked hard to create and sell elegant textiles, and Arachne did not give the gods any credit for their success. She reminded everyone that she and her father were talented on their own, and they worked very hard.

As the goddess of crafts, Athena was outraged to hear Arachne boasting about her weaving skills. Athena came to earth disguised as an old woman and scolded Arachne for not giving credit to the gods for her weaving skills. Arachne just laughed and continued to work on her latest piece. Infuriated,

Athena transformed back into her true form and challenged Arachne to a public weaving contest.

"Gladly!" Arachne accepted.

Athena took clouds from the sky and grass from the ground and wove a tapestry with flattering scenes of the gods reigning on Mount Olympus. Arachne smirked and fashioned her own scene of the gods acting childishly and abusing mortals with their power. Arachne's scenes were so lifelike that they practically leaped off the fabric!

Everyone could see that Arachne's tapestry was the most beautiful, but Athena was enraged. She tore Athena's tapestry to shreds. For daring to insult the gods with her weaving, Athena turned Arachne into the earth's first spider. Arachne would weave webs forever, but she would never see her father again.

DID YOU KNOW?

Weaving was an important skill for women in ancient Greece. They did not usually receive an education, but they did start learning to weave at age five.

SYMBOLS

Arachne is associated with weaving looms and spiders.

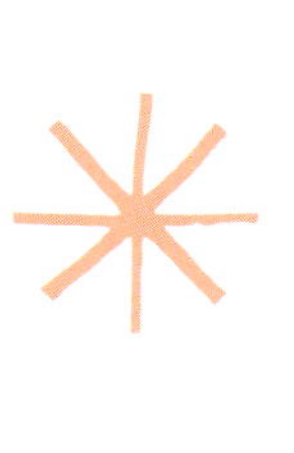

✳ ECHO ✳

Voice of Last Words

Echo was a beautiful wood nymph who loved romance, but she always chose to follow the wrong person. Eventually, she lost everything because of her choices in love.

Zeus, who was married to Hera, had a habit of going to the forest to flirt with wood nymphs. Hera knew that he did this, and she would often try to follow him into the woods and catch him.

Zeus asked Echo to do him a favor. If she saw Hera coming, she was supposed to start talking to Hera to distract her from her mission to find Zeus. Echo would see Hera and then follow her around, chatting and jabbering, until Zeus could escape back to Mount Olympus.

One day, Echo was following Hera around, talking incessantly, and Hera caught a glimpse of Zeus bolting out of the woods.

Hera whirled around and glared at Echo. "I know you're just trying to distract me from finding my husband! I'm so tired of your constant talking!"

She cursed Echo so that Echo could not speak any of her own words ever again. She could only say the last word that someone had said to her.

Echo was devastated, but she caught a glimpse of a gorgeous man named Narcissus next to the river, gazing at his own reflection. She fell in love instantly and tried to get his attention. But she could not speak any of her own words.

Narcissus was looking for his friends and shouted, "Anyone here?" Echo replied, "Here!"

He yelled to his friends, "Come this way!" and Echo said, "This way!"

But Narcissus laughed at her and didn't love her back. Heartbroken, Echo ran away to a cave and sobbed and sobbed. She cried so much that her body wasted away. But still, any time someone shouted in the forest, she echoed their words back to them.

DID YOU KNOW?

In 2014, an acoustic engineer in Manchester, England, created the longest echo sound ever recorded. It was 75 seconds long!

SYMBOLS

Echo is associated with music notes.

CALLIOPE

Muse of Epic Poetry

Calliope is the leader of the Muses, the nine sister goddesses who ruled over the most enjoyable aspects of ancient Greek society, like music, poetry, dance, and knowledge. They were known for their beauty, with teal-colored wings and long violet hair.

The Muses were born on Mount Olympus to Zeus and Mnemosyne, the goddess of memory. Calliope is known as the goddess with the beautiful voice and the goddess of epic poetry. In ancient Greece, poetry was not written down; it was sung. And poems were not necessarily written to express love, but instead to share stories that should be remembered. Mnemosyne remembered the history of the gods, and her daughter Calliope sang them into epic poems, or long stories.

Humans only had creative talents if the Muses gave them creative gifts. Poets needed Calliope to compose songs or plays, so they prayed to her to ask for inspiration.

One day, a group of nine sisters, the daughters of a wealthy landowner named Pierus, decided to challenge the nine Muses to a singing and storytelling contest. The sisters insisted that they were just as talented as the Muses and could sing and tell stories just as well. They chose nymphs to be the judges of the contest. If the Muses lost, they would have to give the sisters two sacred springs. If the sisters lost, they would give up their land.

Calliope swished to the front of the group and tossed her purple hair over her shoulder. She broke into a beautiful song about famous Greek myths, like the stories of Persephone, the nymph Arethusa, and King Lyncus. Her song was so gorgeous that the sisters had no chance of winning.

Angry about losing so badly, the sisters started to insult the Muses. But as they shouted at the Muses, their mouths turned into beaks, their arms turned into wings, and they sprouted black feathers. Calliope turned all nine sisters into magpies for daring to challenge and slander her.

DID YOU KNOW?

The word "museum" means "home of the Muses." Look up the museums in your area and see if there are any interesting exhibits happening!

SYMBOLS

Calliope is associated with tablets, scrolls, and lyres.

CLIO

Muse of History

Clio was the Muse of history, a goddess who could make someone famous. If she recorded your story, you were included in Greek mythology and stories.

Along with her eight other sisters, Clio was a daughter of Zeus and Mnemosyne, the goddess of memory. Like her sister Calliope, the Muse of poetry, Clio's realm of power was connected to memory. Her mother had power over memory, and Clio was in charge of deciding which stories people would remember for centuries to come.

In sculptures and art, Clio is always surrounded by tablets or books. She usually holds a pencil or a scroll, ready to write down the things that were happening around her. She often wears a laurel wreath on her head and a flowing gown. You can easily imagine her studying in your school library with a backpack full of books and a row of neatly sharpened pencils!

While Clio spent a lot of her time writing, one day, she made a mistake and decided to poke fun at Aphrodite, the most beautiful of the goddesses. Aphrodite was married to Hephaestus, but she liked to have other boyfriends, too.

Clio teased Aphrodite for having a crush on a mortal man named Adonis.

Aphrodite could make anyone fall in love, so she cursed Clio to fall in love with a man named Pierus. His nine daughters had insulted Clio and her sisters, so they turned Pierus's daughters into magpies. Now Clio was in love with Pierus and could not control her feelings.

Clio and Pierus had a son named Hyacinth. Hyacinth fell in love with the god Apollo. One day, Hyacinth and Apollo were throwing a discus around for fun, but the discus hit Hyacinth in the head, and he died. Bright purple, pink, and blue flowers sprouted from the ground where his blood spilled, and Apollo named the flowers after Hyacinth. Clio must have appreciated this act of remembrance for her son.

DID YOU KNOW?

The other seven Muses were: Urania, the Muse of astronomy; Thalia, the Muse of comedy; Melpomene, the Muse of tragedy; Polyhymnia, the Muse of religious hymns; Erato, the Muse of love songs; Euterpe, the Muse of lyrical poetry; and Terpsichore, the Muse of dance. Which one would you like to learn more about?

SYMBOLS

Clio is associated with an open scroll and a chest of books.

✳ MEDEA ✳

Sorceress

Medea was the daughter of King Aeëtes and Queen Eidyia. She was part goddess, and she studied with the goddess Hecate to learn everything she needed to know about magic.

Medea fell in love with a prince named Jason who was visiting her kingdom. Jason was supposed to rule Iolcus, a city in Greece, but his half brother took the throne. To become the ruler, Jason needed to find a Golden Fleece, the fleece of a magical ram.

The goddesses Hera and Aphrodite wanted Jason to find this fleece and be the ruler, but they knew he couldn't get the fleece on his own. Aphrodite convinced her son Eros (the god of love) to make Medea fall in love with Jason so that she would use her powers to help him. Medea left her home and joined Jason in his quest.

They boarded a ship called the *Argo* with about fifty men. Jason and his sailors, the Argonauts, met a giant named Talos who kept hurling boulders at their ship. The men were terrified.

Medea summoned spirits from Hades to scare Talos. He was startled and cut his ankle on a sharp rock. As a god, Talos had a substance called ichor in his veins. It bled out of him, and he crashed to the ground like a tree. Medea defeated him while hardly lifting a finger!

Next, Jason was supposed to plow a field using two fire-breathing bulls—impossible! But Medea gave him a protective lotion that made him fireproof for one day. With Medea's magical potion, he finished the task.

Then Jason faced a field full of giant serpent teeth sticking up out of the ground. As if that wasn't scary enough, the teeth turned into skeleton warriors. Jason was afraid, but Medea told him to throw a large boulder at the skeletons. They were distracted and started attacking the boulder. Thanks to Medea, Jason completed another level of his quest.

After Medea and Jason found the Golden Fleece, they married and lived in Corinth. They had two children together, and Medea continued to use her magical powers.

DID YOU KNOW?

There was a famous ancient Greek play about Medea by a man named Euripides. At that time, only men were allowed to watch or act in plays, so the actor in the role of Medea would have been a man.

SYMBOLS

Medea is associated with serpents.

* HECATE *

Goddess of Magic and Ghosts

Hecate was a goddess who could go in and out of different realms, like the earth and the underworld. She used her powers to help humans and other goddesses.

Hecate's parents were minor gods named Perses and Asteria, a goddess of witchcraft. Hecate was usually accompanied by her dogs and always carried a torch. She wore a knee-length dress and hunting boots.

When the goddess Demeter could not find her daughter Persephone, Hecate was the only one who could help her. Hecate was able to see into the underworld and discover that Persephone was being held there by Hades. Hecate guided Demeter into the underworld, lighting the way with her torch so that Demeter could approach Hades.

Since Hecate was able to cross between realms, she also became Persephone's guide in and out of the underworld. She would bring Persephone up to earth in the spring and then in the winter lead her back down into the underworld, where Persephone had to live with Hades.

Hecate also helped train Medea, who famously used her magic to help Jason on his quest for the Golden Fleece. Hecate showed Medea how to gather the herbs that she used to make a fireproof potion for Jason when he fought a fire-breathing bull. The only way to get these herbs was to harvest them from a yellow plant that grew from the blood of a god named Prometheus.

Hecate was a queen of darkness and usually did her work at night. Ancient Greeks who were afraid of the dark could pray to her to ward off evil spirits. Some people also believed that she could help them talk to loved ones in the afterlife or help them get rid of ghosts.

DID YOU KNOW?

Hecate was also often depicted with a pet polecat. Polecats are a European animal that look similar to ferrets.

SYMBOLS

Hecate is associated with twin torches, dogs, and keys to other realms.

THE HARPIES

Half Women, Half Birds

Harpies were half-women, half-bird creatures who were sent by Zeus to torture and punish humans. Their name means "snatchers," and they would snatch things away from humans.

The Harpies were daughters of the gods Thaumas and Electra, like their sister Iris, the rainbow goddess. They originally took the form of the wind, but then they morphed into bird-women. Just as the wind has the power to blow something right out of your grasp, the Harpies also took things away from people.

One of their most famous assignments was a man named Phineus. He was the king of Thrace, near modern-day Turkey. Apollo, the god of prophecy, taught Phineus prophecy skills. Humans like Phineus who could understand prophecies were called seers. Seers were supposed to give guidance to humans but not reveal too much information.

As a seer, Phineus gave too much information to humankind, so Zeus punished him with blindness. Now he could not see the physical world or the world of the gods. Zeus sent the Harpies to torture Phineus.

Anytime a plate of food was placed in front of Phineus, the Harpies swooped down and snatched the food with their talons. If they were too tired to grab the food, they would just drop bird poop on it so that he couldn't eat it. Phineus had no way to defeat the Harpies.

One day, Jason and the Argonauts arrived at Phineus's house on their journey to find the Golden Fleece. Phineus told them how awful his life was because he was tortured by the Harpies every day and couldn't eat anything. As they all sat down to dinner, the Harpies flew in to swipe Phineus's food.

Some of Jason's soldiers chased them off and tried to kill them. Iris, the rainbow goddess, stopped the soldiers and protected her sisters. The Harpies decided they had tortured Phineus for long enough, but they were always ready for their next victim.

DID YOU KNOW?

There is a well-preserved vase from 480 BCE with an image of the Harpies with their bird wings and human faces at the Getty Villa in Malibu, California. You can visit it in person or look at it on their website.

SYMBOLS

The Harpies are associated with birds and wind.

* PSYCHE *

Goddess of the Soul

Psyche was a princess who became a goddess because of the power of her love.

Psyche was so beautiful that Aphrodite, the goddess of beauty, became jealous of her. Aphrodite wanted Psyche to pay a terrible price.

Aphrodite devised a plan. Her son Eros, the god of love, would shoot Psyche with an arrow, causing her to fall in love with a hideous monster. But the plan went off course when Eros drew his bow to shoot Psyche, and he accidentally pricked his own finger and fell desperately in love with her.

Eros brought Psyche to a beautiful mountainside home that magically provided everything she could ever need. Because he was a god, he knew that if Psyche looked at him, she would be cursed. So he only came to her at night when it was dark.

At first, Psyche was confused. But they talked every night in the dark, and, without even seeing him, Psyche fell deeply in love with Eros, too.

One night, Psyche couldn't stand the suspense any longer. She lit an oil lamp so she could see the face of her love. As she glimpsed Eros's handsome face, a drop of oil seared his skin, and he jumped up and ran away, trying to protect Psyche.

Psyche was desperate to find Eros, but Aphrodite had captured him, still furious that her plan hadn't worked. She sent Psyche on impossible missions to distract her from finding Eros. For example, she gave Psyche an enormous pile of mixed seeds and told her to sort them by morning. Psyche didn't think she would ever be able to do it, but insects helped her complete the task.

Psyche's love for Eros motivated her to conquer the obstacles that Aphrodite put in her way. Eros finally escaped from Aphrodite and decided that he never wanted to be away from Psyche ever again. He gave her a drink of ambrosia, the drink of the gods, which made her immortal. She became a goddess and lived with Eros at her side for eternity.

DID YOU KNOW?

The name Psyche means "soul," and was probably a prophecy that her soul would live forever. Today, we use the word "psyche" to mean a human's spirit, mind, or innermost self.

SYMBOLS

Psyche is associated with butterflies. (Psyche means "butterfly" as well as "soul.")

DANAE

Princess of Argos

Danae was the princess of Argos, a wealthy Greek city-state. She later became the mother of one of the most famous Greek **demigods**, Perseus.

Danae's father, King Acrisius, had been told a prophecy that his grandson would kill him. He locked Danae in a tower so that she would never fall in love with anyone or have a baby.

However, Zeus fell in love with Danae and sneaked into her tower by transforming himself into a gold liquid that could slip through the bars. He was the only man—well, god, technically—Danae had seen in a long time. She fell in love with him, too, and they had a baby boy named Perseus.

King Acrisius was shocked when he heard a baby's cries coming from Danae's tower! He ran to find Danae. He couldn't bring himself to kill her son, so he locked Danae and Perseus in a wooden chest and threw them into the Aegean Sea.

Danae cradled Perseus in her arms as they floated and bobbed over the waves. They couldn't see where they were going, but soon they felt their chest wash ashore. Danae heard someone unlocking the chest and braced herself for whoever had found them.

A man named Dictys was surprised to see a gorgeous woman and baby boy inside the chest! He introduced himself and said they were on an island called Seriphos. Danae was relieved to be far away from her father. Dictys was kind. He helped Danae raise Perseus on the beautiful island.

Dictys's brother, Polydectes, was the king of Seriphos. One day, he met Danae and fell instantly in love with her. He wanted to steal her away, but her son Perseus was now a strong young man loyal to Dictys.

Polydectes wanted to get rid of Perseus so that he could have Danae all to himself, so he sent Perseus on a quest to bring him the head of a Gorgon named Medusa. Danae watched her son set off on his journey, but she knew she would see him again one day.

DID YOU KNOW?

A Greek man named Herodotus wrote down a lot of history about Danae's homeland, Argos. Herodotus is remembered today as the "the father of history."

SYMBOLS

Danae is associated with a bronze tower.

✳ MEDUSA ✳

Gorgon

Medusa was a beautiful young woman with long, lustrous hair who gained the power to turn any man who looked at her into stone.

Medusa was the daughter of a sea-god named Phorcys and his sister Ceto, but somehow she was mortal. She had a beautiful face and long pretty hair. One day, the sea-god Poseidon fell in love with Medusa and chased her through a meadow.

Athena, the goddess of wisdom and war, was watching Poseidon as he got closer to Medusa. Some people think that Athena was jealous of Medusa in this moment, but she might have been trying to help her.

Athena transformed Medusa's distinctive hair into snakes and gave her the power to turn anyone who looked at her into stone. Medusa was now a Gorgon, a type of monster with snakes for hair. She was safe from Poseidon, at least for now.

Gorgon Medusa also had wings and wore a knee-length skirt and tight boots. She wore lots of bracelets on her wrists. She spent her days with her two sisters, who were also Gorgons.

Meanwhile, Danae's son Perseus had been given the task of bringing Medusa's head back to Polydectes, the king of Seriphos. Medusa, however, was much more powerful than this demigod. Perseus needed help from many other gods to collect enough weapons to sneak up on Medusa while she slept. He had winged shoes, an invisibility hat, a shield, and a powerful sword.

Perseus sneaked into Medusa's lair and saw that she was fast asleep. He used the shield like a mirror so that he could see Medusa without looking directly at her. He cut off her head with his sword and took it with him. Medusa never had a chance to fight back.

Even though Medusa had been decapitated, she still had power. Perseus flew around with her head and used it as a weapon to turn his enemies into stone.

DID YOU KNOW?

A man named Polygnotos painted a vase with an image of Perseus preparing to attack Medusa, who is sleeping peacefully and barefoot. You can see it at the Metropolitan Museum of Art in New York or on their website.

SYMBOLS

Medusa is associated with snakes.

✳ ANDROMEDA ✳

Ethiopian Princess

Andromeda grew up as a princess in Ethiopia, a kingdom south of Greece. Her father was King Cepheus and her mother was Queen Cassiopeia.

Andromeda's mother, Queen Cassiopeia, talked about her daughter's beauty all the time. She even dared to say that Andromeda was more beautiful than the nereids, sea nymphs who served the sea-god Poseidon.

Poseidon was furious that Cassiopeia dared to compare her daughter to his sea nymphs. In his anger, he flooded Ethiopia with the waters of the Indian Ocean so that he could send a sea monster to devour everyone in the kingdom.

King Cepheus was desperate to save his people. He asked an oracle what he could do. The oracle told him that he must tie Andromeda to a cliff so the sea monster could take her instead of destroying Ethiopia. Full of sadness, King Cepheus agreed to the plan.

Andromeda was terrified! She saw the enormous, sharp-fanged sea monster headed straight for her. She closed her eyes and prayed to the gods to save her.

Suddenly, a young man flew above her on a winged white horse. Perseus had heard Andromeda's cries and came to rescue her. He was riding on his flying horse Pegasus, who had been born from Medusa's blood when Perseus killed her.

Perseus killed the sea monster and asked Andromeda to marry him. She accepted his proposal and they started their journey back to Greece to start their new life. Whenever they met enemies, Perseus turned them to stone with the head of Medusa that he still carried in his bag.

Andromeda and Perseus ruled the kingdom of Mycenae and had three sons and three daughters together. They lived happily for many years. Athena wanted to reward Andromeda for being a good wife to Perseus, so she placed Andromeda among the stars when she died. The Andromeda constellation is named for her.

DID YOU KNOW?

Because Ethiopia is near the equator, people there can see constellations in both the northern and southern hemispheres. Andromeda and her parents Cepheus and Cassiopeia all have their own constellations named after them. Can you find them in the sky where you live?

SYMBOLS

Andromeda is associated with the Andromeda constellation.

✳ ATALANTA ✳

Heroine of Arcadia

In addition to being a princess, Atalanta was the fastest runner and the best hunter in Arcadia.

Atalanta was the daughter of King Iasus of Arcadia. King Iasus wanted a son, so he abandoned her in the wilderness. Baby Atalanta cried out. A brown bear heard and rescued Atalanta.

Raised by bears in the wilderness, Atalanta learned to hunt and run very fast. The people of Greece started to hear stories about what an amazing hunter she was.

A great hunter named Meleager asked her to help him kill a giant boar, who had tusks longer than an elephant. His other men laughed when they saw Atalanta joining their team. But suddenly, the boar came charging through the woods. The men fumbled with their weapons, but Atalanta calmly raised her bow and shot the boar in the heart.

Atalanta caught the eye of the goddess of hunting, Artemis, who also loved to be out in the wilderness. Artemis and Atalanta spent their time hunting in the forest and had no interest in getting married or having children.

When Atalanta's father Iasus heard of her fame and skills, he brought her back to the palace and begged for her forgiveness. Atalanta agreed to return to Arcadia as a princess.

Iasus forced Atalanta to choose a husband. Atalanta decided to have a race. Anyone who wanted to marry her would have to beat her to the finish line. If the men lost the race, they would lose their life. Only very brave—or very arrogant—men competed for her hand in marriage.

One by one, Atalanta beat the fastest men in Arcadia. Then a man named Hippomenes stepped up to the starting line. Atalanta was beating him, but the goddess Aphrodite had given him three golden apples. Hippomenes threw down one golden apple, distracting Atalanta, but she was still in the lead. He threw down another, and finally a third. Atalanta stopped to pick it up, and Hippomenes won the race.

Atalanta agreed to marry the clever and quick Hippomenes and still remained a heroine to the Arcadians.

DID YOU KNOW?

Atalanta's name sounds like the Greek word for "equal in weight." Do you think this connects to her story in any way?

SYMBOLS

Atalanta is associated with bears, bows and arrows, and golden apples.

CALLISTO

Princess of Arcadia

Callisto was the princess of Arcadia, a rural area of ancient Greece. Her father King Lycaon was an evil man, so Zeus turned him into a wolf to punish him.

No longer safe in the palace, Callisto decided to dedicate herself to the goddess Artemis and live in the woods. She loved spending her days with Artemis and the wood nymphs, taking care of animals and protecting the forest.

One day, Zeus realized how beautiful Callisto was and wanted to be with her. But since he had turned her father into a wolf, Callisto did not trust Zeus. Knowing this, Zeus disguised himself as Artemis so that he could spend time with her.

Zeus placed a spell on Callisto so that she became pregnant. As a maiden who served Artemis, Callisto was not supposed to marry or have babies. Callisto tried to hide the pregnancy, but eventually Artemis noticed. Artemis sent her away.

Callisto cried as she turned away from Artemis and her other friends. She found her own corner of the woods and gave birth to a son named Arcas. She loved Arcas very much.

One day, while Callisto was playing with baby Arcas in the woods, she was suddenly face-to-face with the goddess Hera. Hera, Zeus's wife, was jealous of Callisto and Arcas, who was Zeus's son. In her anger, Hera turned Callisto into a bear. Callisto was devastated that she wouldn't get to raise her son, but she remained in the woods so that she could see him whenever he went there.

When Arcas was a teenager, he became a good hunter. One day, he was hunting quietly and came upon a brown bear. He pulled back his bow and steadied his arrow to shoot the bear.

Zeus looked down just in time to see that Arcas was about to shoot Callisto! He swooped down and stopped Arcas, feeling sorry that Hera had turned Callisto into a bear. Zeus decided to turn Callisto and Arcas into stars so that they could be together forever.

DID YOU KNOW?

Callisto's and Arcas's constellations are called Ursa Major and Ursa Minor. They are also known as Big Bear and Little Bear, and they share stars with the Big Dipper and Little Dipper. Research tips on how to locate them in the night sky!

SYMBOLS

Callisto is associated with bears and stars.

SPHINX OF THEBES

Keeper of Riddles

The Sphinx, a woman with eagle wings and the body of a lion, told a riddle to anyone brave enough to hear it. If they could not answer her riddle, they would die.

The goddess Hera sent the Sphinx to the city of Thebes to punish them for ancient crimes against her. There were stories of Sphinxes from as far south as Egypt, and they were popular in Greek stories as well. The Sphinx of Thebes was the daughter of a monster named Typhoeus and Echidna, who was half woman and half snake.

Foolish young men of Thebes often approached the Sphinx, convinced that they were clever enough to solve her riddle. She asked them, "What creature walks on four legs in the morning, two legs at noon, and three in the evening?" No one could solve the riddle, and they were struck dead when they failed.

Creon, the leader of Thebes, wanted the Sphinx out of his city. He was tired of her striking down young men who could serve in his army. He decided to raise the stakes to attract the smartest and bravest men in Thebes.

He offered his sister Jocasta as a wife to anyone who could solve the riddle. Her husband Laius had just died, and whoever she married next would become king of Thebes.

A young man named Oedipus had recently arrived in Thebes. He grew up in Corinth but had received a very scary prophecy from an oracle, so he ran away to avoid his fate. He had nothing to lose and decided to try to solve the Sphinx's riddle.

The Sphinx told Oedipus her riddle, and he frowned while he thought about the answer. Suddenly, the riddle became clear to him, and he told the Sphinx the correct answer.

The Sphinx was furious that Oedipus solved the riddle. She ran away to the mountains. However, she still had power over Oedipus. He thought he was escaping his prophecy, but by marrying Jocasta and becoming the king of Thebes, he helped his own prophecy come true.

DID YOU KNOW?

Did you solve the Riddle of the Sphinx? It's a human! We crawl on four legs in the beginning of our lives, then walk on two legs, then use a cane like a third leg in old age.

SYMBOLS

The Sphinx is associated with the book of riddles, wings, and lions.

ARIADNE

Princess of Crete

Ariadne was the princess of the island of Crete, where a deadly monster lived in a cage beneath her palace. She helped defeat him.

Ariadne's father, King Minos, conquered the Greek city of Athens. Every year, he demanded that the Athenians send him seven boys and seven girls. He sacrificed the children to the **Minotaur**, a half-man, half-bull monster who lived beneath the palace. The Minotaur lived in a **labyrinth**, an inescapable maze that trapped both the Minotaur and the children who were sacrificed.

Theseus, the prince of Athens, was determined to kill the Minotaur and stop these sacrifices. He volunteered to go to Crete as one of the seven boys.

Ariadne was looking out the window of the palace when the ship with the Athenians arrived. She caught sight of the handsome Prince Theseus and fell in love. She could not let him be killed by the Minotaur!

When it was dark, Ariadne sneaked out of her room and found Theseus. The young prince and princess talked all night and fell in love. They wanted to run away to Athens and get married, but first they would have to defeat the Minotaur.

Ariadne came up with a plan. She gave Theseus a ball of string and told him to tie one end to the entrance of the labyrinth so that he would be able to follow it and find his way out of the maze.

The next morning, King Minos's guards shoved the fourteen kids into the labyrinth. While the rest of the kids tried to hide, Theseus went looking for the Minotaur. The giant monster had the body of a man with the head of a bull, including huge horns. Theseus ran through the maze, making the Minotaur dizzy. Theseus suddenly spun around and slashed the Minotaur's neck with his sword. He followed the string and led the other Athenian kids back to the entrance.

King Minos was furious that Theseus had killed his monster, but Ariadne and Theseus rushed to board a boat back to Athens and avoid his wrath. Ariadne's quick thinking had saved the prince.

DID YOU KNOW?

Years later, Ariadne married Dionysus, the god of wine and parties. He loved her so much that he made her immortal, and she went to live among the gods.

SYMBOLS

Ariadne is associated with thread, labyrinths, and crowns.

✳ NEMESIS ✳

Goddess of Retribution

The gods did not like it when humans became too proud or overconfident. The goddess Nemesis made sure that humans didn't forget that they should rely on the gods for everything.

If a human became too proud of their own skills, the gods called it **hubris**. Nemesis watched over humans to make sure that they were not getting too arrogant. If they did, she was in charge of retribution, or payback.

One famous example of hubris is the story of Icarus. His father was Daedalus, a famous inventor. Daedalus invented wings from feathers and beeswax that allowed humans to fly. Icarus was excited. Thanks to his father's invention, he could fly just like a god! Daedalus warned Icarus not to fly too close to the sun, because the wax would melt and the wings would fall apart.

Nemesis was surely watching unhappily as Icarus swooped and soared through the clouds. He was having the time of his life! Suddenly, his wings began to droop and he lost his momentum. The wings collapsed on his back, and he fell to his death. Daedalus regretted giving his son a godlike experience for the rest of his life.

Nemesis was powerful, but Zeus made sure that she knew her proper place in the gods' world. One day, Zeus caught sight of Nemesis and wanted to be with her. Like so many women before her, Nemesis did not want anything to do with Zeus, so she tried to hide from him by turning herself into a goose. Zeus turned himself into a swan and caught her.

Nemesis laid an egg, and Zeus gave the egg to the Queen of Sparta, Leda. When the egg hatched, a baby girl named Helen was born. She was the princess of Sparta and very beautiful. Later on, Zeus would use Helen to teach the humans a lesson about hubris during the Trojan War.

The English word "nemesis" is based on the goddess Nemesis. It means "the cause of someone's downfall," just like Nemesis would cause the downfall of those who were too proud.

DID YOU KNOW?

Have you ever heard the warning, "Don't fly too close to the sun"? This English saying is an allusion, or a reference, to the story of Icarus.

SYMBOLS

Nemesis is associated with apple branches and balances or scales.

ERIS

Goddess of Arguments

Eris was the least popular of the gods because she loved to cause trouble for both gods and humans.

One day, the gods threw a wedding party for a king named Peleus and the sea nymph Thetis. They invited all the gods—except for Eris. Eris always caused fights and drama at parties, so they didn't want to include her.

Eris was furious. She stomped her foot, put on a party dress, and started thinking about how she could ruin the festivities.

She knew that the other goddesses were vain and loved to use a party to show off their beauty. They were also jealous of anyone else's beauty. Suddenly, Eris knew exactly what to do.

Eris crashed the party holding a shiny golden apple. She had written "for the fairest" in cursive script on the apple. Eris saw Hera, Athena, and Aphrodite talking and laughing together, twirling their dresses and tossing their hair over their shoulders.

Eris slowly rolled the golden apple toward the goddesses. "So, girls, who is the most beautiful?" she asked. They eyed each other suspiciously. Eris said that a mortal named Paris would judge a competition to determine who was the most beautiful goddess. Hera, Athena, and Aphrodite each tried to convince Paris that they should be the winner.

Aphrodite, the goddess of love, knew that the best way to win over a mortal man was to offer him a beautiful mortal woman. She promised Paris that if he chose her as the most beautiful goddess, she would give him the most beautiful woman as his wife.

Paris agreed to her plan. Aphrodite won the golden apple, and then she helped Paris kidnap Helen of Sparta, the most beautiful woman on earth. Helen was already married to King Menelaus, so her disappearance enraged him!

Eris couldn't have been happier. The goddesses were still mad at each other, and now the humans were preparing to go to war over the kidnapping of a queen. She was pleased with herself for causing arguments in the heavens and on earth!

DID YOU KNOW?

Ares, the god of war, was Eris's brother. Why do you think mythology connected these two figures?

SYMBOLS

Eris is associated with golden apples and snakes.

HELEN

Queen of Sparta

The Greeks blamed Helen's beauty for the longest and most deadly war in their history. But Helen defended herself and argued that she was simply used by the gods to cause destruction.

From the time Helen was young, people had used her beauty as a tool to get what they wanted. She was the princess of Sparta, the daughter of King Tyndareus and Queen Leda. Word of Helen's beauty spread far and wide, so there were many princes and kings who wanted to marry her.

Her father knew that any man who did not get to marry Helen might turn on Sparta and become their enemy. So he made the suitors sign a contract that said even if they didn't get to marry Helen, they would defend her in battle if she ever needed it. This way, Helen would find a husband, and Sparta would end up with a large backup army.

Helen chose a man named Menelaus, and together they ruled Sparta. They had a daughter named Hermione. Helen was happy with her life in Sparta until one day, a man named Paris from Troy (in modern-day Turkey) kidnapped her with the help of Aphrodite.

The men who had vowed to protect Helen now had to fight to get Helen back. The Greeks and Trojans fought for ten years, and many men died on both sides.

Paris died in the fighting, and Helen was forced to marry his brother Deiphobus. But after Menelaus and his army conquered Troy, he killed Deiphobus and took Helen back to Sparta.

Everyone blamed Helen for the war. They said that her face was so beautiful that it "launched a thousand ships" into battle.

But Helen defended herself. She said that the gods planned the war because the earth was getting too full of humans. They wanted to get rid of a lot of people at once. Helen blamed Aphrodite for helping Paris kidnap her, knowing that this would cause a war. Helen's beauty was powerful, but she knew that it was the gods who actually caused destruction, not her.

DID YOU KNOW?

In 415 BCE, Euripides wrote a play called *The Trojan Women* that highlights Helen's perspective on the story of the Trojan War. You can find recordings of modern-day adaptations of the play on YouTube!

SYMBOLS

Helen is associated with the Apple of Discord, ships, and mirrors.

PENTHESILEA

Queen of the Amazon Warriors

Penthesilea was the queen of a tribe of women called the Amazons. As daughters of Ares, the god of war, they were fierce warriors who often fought against the Greeks.

Only women lived in the Amazon community. Sometimes they traveled to fight or explore, and the women would fall in love and become pregnant. If they had a baby boy, they left him with the father. If they had a baby girl, they took her back with them to live with the tribe.

Amazons always fought together, usually in groups of twelve or more.

Penthesilea, the Amazon queen, invented a bladed axe weapon that the Amazons used to fight. She and the Amazons decided to join Priam, the king of Troy, in his war against the Greeks.

The goddess Athena was rooting for the Greeks in the Trojan War, so she cast a spell on Penthesilea. She sent a dream to trick her, telling her to fight Achilles, the best Greek warrior. In her dream, Penthesilea won the battle.

Penthesilea woke up the next day and dressed in shining gold body armor. She held her double-pointed axe, a gift from the goddess Eris. Penthesilea and the Amazons marched into battle and immediately took down Greek soldiers. Penthesilea made a list of the many men that she killed.

The soldiers were shouting and crying out so loudly that Achilles came to see what was happening. He saw their leader, Penthesilea, and charged to fight her. Achilles had the gods on his side, and he threw his spear at Penthesilea. It pierced her armor, and she fell to the ground.

Achilles saw that he had killed a great warrior and was sorry for what he had done. He gave Penthesilea's body back to the Trojans, and they honored her with an expensive hero's funeral. Penthesilea was one of the great warriors of the Trojan War.

DID YOU KNOW?

The Amazons were the second-most-popular figures on Greek pottery, after Heracles. There are thousands of vases with Amazons painted on them, now in museums all over the world.

SYMBOLS

Penthesilea is associated with armor, weapons, and double-headed axes.

CASSANDRA

Prophetess and Princess of Troy

Cassandra had the gift of prophecy and tried to warn her people about the Trojan War. If they had listened to her, they could have saved many lives.

Cassandra was the princess of Troy. Her father was King Priam, and her brother was Prince Paris. She was incredibly beautiful and caught the eye of Apollo, the god of prophecy. He gave Cassandra the gift of prophecy, or telling the future, hoping that it would make her fall in love with him.

However, Cassandra turned him down, and Apollo regretted giving her the gift. He couldn't take it back, so he put a curse on everyone in Troy. Cassandra could tell prophecies, but no one in Troy would believe her.

Cassandra had a vision that her brother Paris would cause a horrible war in Troy. When he set out to kidnap Helen of Sparta, Cassandra begged King Priam not to let him go. But Priam and Paris ignored her. After Paris brought Helen back with him, all of Greece set out to invade Troy, and the Trojan War began, just as Cassandra had predicted.

During the fighting, Cassandra also had a vision about a giant wooden horse. She warned her father to be wary of anything that looked like what she saw in her vision. But one day, a large wooden horse showed up outside the gates of Troy. It had a note attached to it that said it was a Greek offering to the goddess Athena.

The Trojans decided that they would steal the offering from the Greeks, so they brought it inside the city gates. Cassandra insisted that it was a trick, but no one would listen to her. In the middle of the night, Greek soldiers crawled out of the giant horse and attacked the sleeping Trojan soldiers. A Greek soldier named Odysseus had come up with the plan, and, because no one listened to Cassandra's warning, the plan worked.

Cassandra was the wisest woman in Troy, but because no one listened to her, her people lost the Trojan War.

DID YOU KNOW?

The tale of the Trojan War is one of the oldest and greatest stories in the world, and there are many different adaptations of it. Find a modern version for kids at your local library or bookstore!

SYMBOLS

Cassandra is associated with mirrors (to see the future) and torches (to light the way).

✳ CIRCE ✳

Sorceress of Aeaea

Circe was a skilled sorceress. She lived on her own personal island with nymphs, wolves, and lions for company, and she cast spells on anyone who arrived there.

Circe's father was the sun-god Helios, and he gave her a magic wand with a shining sun on the end. Her mother was a minor goddess named Perse.

After the Greeks won the Trojan War, a hero named Odysseus was traveling back to his home in Ithaca with his soldiers. They landed on the shores of Aeaea, hoping to rest and eat. Odysseus sent a few men out to explore the island.

Circe was not happy to see the dirty, smelly soldiers show up on her island. But she realized that she was outnumbered and would not be able to fight them off. She decided to trick the soldiers.

"Welcome!" Circe shouted as she approached the men on the beach. "Come to my house, it's just up the path. I'll give you dinner and a place to rest." The group of men hurried up to her large stone house.

Circe secretly poured a few drops of a potion into the drinks before she served them to the soldiers. The men slurped down the drinks and hungrily ate her food. Circe tapped her magic wand at them and they all turned into pigs! She put them in a pigpen behind her house.

When the men didn't return, Odysseus set out to find them. As he was making his way to Circe's house, the messenger god Hermes stopped him and gave him a potion that would block any spells Circe cast on him.

When Circe tried to turn Odysseus into a pig, nothing happened. Circe knew he must have had powerful magic protecting him, so she made a deal with him. She agreed to turn his soldiers back into men, and they all became friends. Odysseus and his men stayed at Circe's house for a year before continuing on their journey.

Odysseus and Circe had a son named Telegonus. Circe raised him on her enchanted island.

DID YOU KNOW?

The name Circe means to "hoop around," which is a reference to the way her spells would encircle her targets.

SYMBOLS

Circe is associated with a wand with a sun on the tip and lions.

THE SIRENS

Singing Winged Women

No one could resist the song of the Sirens. They lived along the coast and sang so beautifully that ships would crash on their shores as sailors tried to reach them.

The Sirens were daughters of the Muse of dancing and singing, Terpsichore, and the river god Achelous. They were originally handmaidens who served the goddess Persephone when she was young.

After Persephone was kidnapped, the Sirens moved to an island that was in a common path for ships sailing to and from Greece. The Sirens played lyres and sang beautiful songs that sailors passing by couldn't resist. The songs would put them in a trance, and the sailors would steer their ships toward the rocky shores of the island. The ships would crash, and the Sirens would take their food and supplies. They were happy living on their island with a constant supply of resources.

Circe lived nearby on her own island, and she knew that her new friend Odysseus would have to pass by the Sirens as he continued on his journey home. As Odysseus and his men set out to sea, Circe warned him to put beeswax in the sailors' ears so that their ship wouldn't be destroyed by the Sirens' song.

Odysseus took Circe's advice and put beeswax in the sailors' ears. He wanted to hear the song for himself, though. He strapped himself to the mast of the ship for safety as they passed the island. When he heard the Sirens' song, he couldn't resist it!

"Please!" he begged his men. "Untie me and go to the island! I must get to the Sirens!" But his men couldn't hear him with the beeswax in their ears, and they sailed past the island.

Circe's advice saved Odysseus and his men. The Sirens were disappointed to miss out on Odysseus's ship, but they only had to wait for the next ship to pass by.

DID YOU KNOW?

There was a Greek artist in the 470s BCE who was simply known as the Siren Painter. He decorated many vases with different scenes featuring Sirens. You can see some of them at the British Museum.

SYMBOLS

The Sirens are associated with wings and lyres.

CALYPSO

Island Goddess of Ogygia

Calypso's name means "I will hide you." She tried to hide the Greek hero Odysseus on her island to keep him for herself.

Calypso lived in a cave on an island called Ogygia. It was full of trees, vines, and lovely meadows. Her father was Atlas, one of the younger Titan gods.

After Odysseus left Circe's island and successfully made it past the Sirens, his men found some cattle on the island of Thrinacia. They ate the cattle and offered some as a sacrifice, and then continued on their journey. They didn't realize that the cattle belonged to the sun-god Helios, and they were punished by the gods. Their ship was destroyed in a storm, and every soldier drowned—except Odysseus.

Calypso watched the shipwreck from a hill on her island. She decided that she was lonely on the island, and she wanted to keep a sailor for company. She saw Odysseus clinging to a piece of wood, trying to make it to safety.

Calypso helped Odysseus to shore and showed him around her island. She grew black poplar trees and violets in her garden.

She had pet owls, seagulls, and hawks that flew around and kept her company. Odysseus was nervous, because he knew that those birds represented death.

But Calypso was kind to Odysseus. She cooked him food and gave him a warm place to live and sleep. She fell in love with Odysseus and lived with him for seven years. She wanted him to live on her island forever, so she offered to make him immortal.

Odysseus had a wife waiting for him in Ithaca. He declined Calypso's offer, and she was heartbroken and jealous of his wife, Penelope.

Athena knew how violent goddesses could be when they were jealous, so she decided to intervene. She sent the messenger god Hermes to convince Calypso to let Odysseus go.

Calypso finally agreed, and she built Odysseus a raft from the trees on her island. He set off alone, one step closer to home.

DID YOU KNOW?

Odysseus is one of the rare humans who declines an offer to become immortal. Do you think he made the right choice?

SYMBOLS

Calypso is associated with the sea, trees, and hawks.

PENELOPE

Queen of Ithaca

Penelope ruled Ithaca for twenty years while her husband Odysseus fought in the Trojan War and then tried to get home.

Penelope and Odysseus were a happy couple who reigned over Ithaca. They had a young son named Telemachus. Soon after they married, however, all the leaders in Greece were called to fight the Trojans.

The Trojan War lasted for ten years. When Odysseus didn't come home, Penelope's parents assumed he was dead and urged her to remarry.

More than one hundred suitors showed up to Penelope's palace, hoping to win her hand in marriage. But she didn't want to marry any of them. She tried to find a way to delay.

She told her suitors that she needed time to weave a shawl for her father-in-law. All good Greek women spent a lot of their time weaving, and she was doing a good deed for Odysseus's father, so everyone agreed to her plan. But the suitors started to get restless after three years when the shawl was not finished.

Penelope worked on the shawl during the day when people could see her, but she secretly unraveled her work at night. They finally realized she had tricked them. Penelope needed a new plan.

She gave the suitors a challenge. Whoever could take Odysseus's bow and shoot an arrow through an impossibly narrow row of axe-heads would get to marry her. If they all failed, then she would be free to continue to wait for Odysseus.

Man after man failed the challenge. Suddenly, an old man who looked like a beggar stepped up and drew back the bow and arrow. He let the arrow fly perfectly through the row of axe-heads. When he turned to Penelope, she saw his true face—it was Odysseus! He was grateful to Penelope for waiting for him to return. Penelope used her wisdom to keep the country running for twenty years, and then cleverly avoided being trapped into a marriage she didn't want.

DID YOU KNOW?

In 1886, Dora Wheeler created a tapestry that showed Penelope unweaving her work at night. It is an especially interesting art piece because it is woven, just like Penelope's shawl. You can see it at the Metropolitan Museum of Art website.

SYMBOLS

Penelope is associated with looms.

SAPPHO

Great Greek Poet

Sappho was a famous songwriter in her lifetime, and she is still one of the most famous ancient writers today. Her fans called her the "tenth Muse."

Sappho was born around 630 BCE on a Greek island called Lesbos. Her family was wealthy, so she had more opportunities for education and self-expression than most Greek women did. She was surrounded by a creative culture from a young age.

Like most young Greek women, Sappho learned to weave as a girl. Weaving was her first form of creative expression, and she used her tapestries to tell stories.

Sappho was multitalented. She wrote all kinds of songs and poems. She wrote blessings to the gods, wedding songs, funeral songs, and long stories called epics. She sang her verses to a tune while she played her lyre. She became most famous for love songs with romantic lyrics about women and men.

When she grew up, Sappho married a wealthy merchant, and together they had a daughter, Cleïs, named after Sappho's mother.

Sappho opened a school for girls to learn poetry and music. She taught young women to write and play music like she did. It disappointed her when her students got married before they finished their education. She wrote sad songs for girls who married young and gave up their artistic talents.

She was the first Greek poet to write from her own point of view and use the word "I." Most poets, like Homer, wrote about other people, mostly Greek gods and heroes. Sappho's writings talked about her own life and what women thought about and dreamed about in ancient Greece.

Although most of Sappho's writings have been lost over more than two thousand years, we still have many of her lyrics. She continues to inspire people with her heartfelt, emotional writing. In a way, her writing has made her immortal.

DID YOU KNOW?

One of Sappho's lyrics talks about "crowns of violets and roses," so Sappho fans often wore purple flower crowns in their hair, and still do today.

SYMBOLS

Sappho is associated with violets, purple, and wings.

ASPASIA

Wisest Woman in Athens

Some of the most famous thinkers in Greek history—Plato, Socrates, and Pericles—all admired the ideas of one brilliant woman named Aspasia of Melitus.

The fifth century BCE was known as the Golden Age of Athens. This was a time when Athens was very wealthy. They built beautiful monuments, and their government began to look like the democracy that we see today. The man who received credit for many of these achievements was Pericles, one of the most famous politicians in Athenian history.

But Pericles didn't come up with all of his ideas on his own. A woman named Aspasia of Melitus had a major influence on him.

Aspasia was born around 470 BCE in a Greek city called Melitus and moved to Athens when she was about twenty. She met Pericles there, and he fell madly in love with her. Aspasia and Pericles were a famous couple in Athens. Everyone knew how much they loved each other.

Aspasia was highly educated and very intelligent. She taught lessons on public speaking, a valuable skill in ancient Athens. People shared their ideas in a public space called the **agora**.

It was important to be able to express your ideas in a clear, convincing, and entertaining speech.

Socrates, who is considered one of the smartest men in history, would visit her just to hear her ideas and ask her questions. He brought along his students to learn from her as well. Socrates encouraged his friends' wives to go take her classes about public speaking.

Another famous scholar named Plato admired Aspasia for her public speaking skills. He said that she was very good at planning out her speeches and also improvising to make them more interesting.

In the 420s, Athens fought against Sparta in the famous Peloponnesian War. About a third of the people of Athens died, including Pericles, the love of Aspasia's life. Historians are not sure when Aspasia died, but in her lifetime she was one of the most famous women in Athens.

DID YOU KNOW?

Sometimes women are left out of the most important stories in history. Can you think of any women like Aspasia who had a major impact on history or politics?

SYMBOLS

Aspasia is associated with public squares and speaking.

GLOSSARY

AGORA: a public open space used for markets and gatherings in ancient Greece

CHARIOT: a two-wheeled horse-drawn vehicle used in ancient warfare and racing

DEITIES: gods or goddesses

DEMIGOD: a person who is half god and half mortal

DRYAD: a nymph who lives in a forest or in a tree

HEARTH: the brick or stone area in front of a fireplace

HUBRIS: excessive pride or self-confidence

IMMORTAL: a god or goddess who lives forever and does not age

LABYRINTH: a complicated network of passages, a maze

LYRE: a U-shaped stringed instrument like a small harp

MINOTAUR: a monster with the body of a man and the head of a bull

MORTAL: a human being who will age and, one day, die

NYMPH: a mythological spirit of nature, similar to a fairy

ORACLE: a person who provides prophecies or advice about the future

PRIESTESS: a female religious figure who ran the temple, performed rituals, and communicated with the gods

PROPHECY: a prediction about the future that comes true

SACRIFICE: a special gift, often an animal, given to the gods to show them honor and respect, or to ask for their help.

TEMPLE: a special building where gods and goddesses are worshipped

TITANS: a family of giants born of Ouranos and Gaia who ruled the earth before the Olympians overthrew them

UNDERWORLD: the realm where the souls of the dead go after the die. It is ruled by the god Hades.

MORE HEROES TO EXPLORE

CLYTEMNESTRA: the half sister of Helen of Sparta and the wife of King Agamemnon. She is a character in several Greek plays.

ELECTRA: the daughter of King Agamemnon and Queen Clytemnestra of Mycenae. There are two Greek plays written about her.

HYPATIA: one of the smartest women in ancient Greece, an astronomer and mathematician

PHOEBE: one of the twelve Titan children of Gaia and Ouranos and the mother of Leto

PLEIONE: one of the daughters of Tethys and the mother of Calypso

STHENO AND EURYALE: the Gorgon sisters of Medusa who tried to save her from Perseus

TELESILLA OF ARGOS: a poet in ancient Greece. She may have even fought in battles to defend Argos.

TETHYS: another daughter of Gaia and Ouranos. She was the mother of many river gods and Oceanids, or sea nymphs.

THEMIS: another one of the twelve Titan children of Gaia and Ouranos. She was the goddess of justice and order.

TIRESIAS: born as the son of a shepherd and a nymph, but Hera turned her into a woman. She served Hera as a prophet.

RESOURCES

To learn more about Greek gods and goddesses and ancient Greek history, check out these resources:

The British Museum website has a collection of statues, paintings, and plates that depict some of the most famous ancient Greek deities.
britishmuseum.org

The Google Arts & Culture site has high-quality images of statues of all the most famous Greek gods and goddesses.
artsandculture.google.com

The Metropolitan Museum of Art in New York City has an incredible collection of ancient Greek sculptures, vases, and artifacts that depict the gods and goddess. They are breathtaking to see in person, or you can also explore the collection on their website.
metmuseum.org

Ask your parents to play the *Greeking Out* podcast by National Geographic to learn more fun stories about life on Mount Olympus.
nationalgeographic.com/podcasts/greeking-out

Check out more stories of Greek mythology in *Greek Mythology for Kids: Legendary Stories of Gods, Heroes, and Mythological Creatures* by Zachary Hamby.

ACKNOWLEDGMENTS

Thank you so much to my F.A. students during the 2024–2025 school year, who helped keep me motivated and checked on my stress-o-meter every day. You had some great suggestions for goddesses to include in the book, and the disapproving shakes of your heads when I didn't meet a writing goal on time really pushed me to catch up and stay on course. It was so much fun to share this challenge with you.

ABOUT THE AUTHOR

Megan DuVarney Forbes is the author of three history books for students. She teaches middle school history and English and loves to read. She lives in Los Angeles with her husband, son, and daughter. You can find out more about what she is reading, writing, and teaching on her YouTube channel, blog, and Instagram account, all called Too Cool for Middle School. Her favorite Greek goddess is Hestia.

ABOUT THE ILLUSTRATOR

Meel Tamphanon is a freelance illustrator from Phuket. She has worked with various clients including 20th Century Studios, Disney, Magic the Gathering, Wizards of the Coast, *The Boston Globe*, and *Corriere della Sera*. Most of her illustrations aim at narrativity, communication, and intellectual components. Her work is related to the surreal, the mythological, history, children's book illustration, and editorial illustrations. Her style is complex with color combinations and grain textures.

EXPLORE THE SERIES AND MEET EVEN MORE HEROES!

WHOSE STORY WILL INSPIRE YOU?